moving to the clear

JASON DEWINETZ

NEWEST PRESS

Canadian Cataloguing in Publication Data
Dewinetz, Jason, 1970–
Moving to the clear

Poems.

ISBN 1-896300-58-8

I. Title. PS8557.E912M68 2002   C811'.54   C2001-911662-4
PR9199.3.D4915M68 2002

Editor for the Press: Douglas Barbour
Cover photograph: Skan/9
Cover and interior design: Ruth Linka
Author photograph: Jennifer Bogart

THE CANADA COUNCIL LE CONSEIL DES ARTS
FOR THE ARTS DU CANADA
SINCE 1957 DEPUIS 1957

Canadian Patrimoine
Heritage canadien

NeWest Press acknowledges the support of the Canada Council for the Arts and the Alberta Foundation for the Arts for our publishing program. We also acknowledge the financial support of the Government of Canada through the Book Publishing Industry Development Program (BPIDP) for our publishing activities.

Some of these poems first appeared in the following periodicals: "Badlands" and "Undressing for bed" in *Descant*. "If we could just forget how to speak" in *Prairie Fire*. "'About the spiders'" in *PRISM International*. "Morning swim" and "The second dead duck" in *Zygote*. "Géricault's Severed Limbs Paintings" and the "In Theory" poems were first published as chapbooks by Greenboathouse Books and above/ground press, respectively.

Many of these poems are interspersed with fragments of lines from Michael Ondaatje's book *Secular Love*—often, but not always, printed in italics. The Géricault sequence also makes use of lines from Lawrence Eitner's study *Géricault's Raft of the Medusa*. The italicized passage on page 24 is from Tom Waits' song "Swordfishtrombone."

NeWest Press
201–8540–109 Street
Edmonton, Alberta T6G 1E6
(780) 432-9427
www.newestpress.com

1 2 3 4 5 06 05 04 03 02

PRINTED AND BOUND IN CANADA

And that is all this writing should be then.
The beautiful formed things caught at the wrong moment
so they are shapeless, awkward
moving to the clear.

—Michael Ondaatje

Contents

Ω

A guide in the birds of the North Okanagan

. . . or the muscle of heart on her clothesline, held with old wooden pegs.

She sits in a lawn chair with a cold drink set on the armrest,
watching the damp thing thrown back and forth in the wind, pulling at the line.

Pegs so old they're hardly holding at all,

and when the wind picks it up
lifts it simple as leaf or memory,
a swallow darting through poplar boughs,

you just let it go.

Boathouse Journal

Sun turns from a beam of yellow into a haze of white over the hills across the lake. A glare off the slopes that appear almost as snowscape. Veins of dry riverbed now clotted with thick thistle. An all but unnoticed green or brown reflected within the recesses of the lake surface. Slight burst of foam onto the beach. Hands dusty from throwing horseshoes at nothing in the sand, the dock rising slowly with the lake,
late spring.

Have been here two weeks.

Slowly unpacking books, notes, clearing cobwebs from the window while Okanagan sun pleads sloth. Spend most afternoons on the pier, to absorb the breeze across water, and sit slowly lowering chains. Setting them down. Anchor as exaggerated fishhook, eager for skin, for blood maybe. Thought blurring in the heat, twisting dizzy towards afternoon as though standing too quickly.
Turning to find the hallucinated shapes of others.

Have begun to hear the voices of animals as well. To give them voices. Swallows and mallards, grebe, the single bald eagle drifting over the lake two days ago.

Talking to birds now.

The second dead duck

Hammock

A pillow in one hand towards the orange hammock hung between
willow and cottonwood, a copy of *The Diviners* and a rye and coke.

Walking down the gravel driveway,
sort of shaking her head when I see her,
holding her hair in a bun with one hand
somehow broadening this gesture.
Almost, *here we go again.*

Hasn't come by in a week or something like a week.
Have convinced myself I'm not waiting but
have gone hours without a cigarette,
hesitant to drive to the SUPER-SAVE, just in case.

She sits into the hammock and reaches for the blue glass.
Can I have some?
Of course.
What is it.
Rye and coke.
Of course.

Dead Duck

It isn't until later that she puts it into words,
but that damn bird was a sign I should have recognized.

Her tanned foot pushing at the ground as she rocks us back and
forth, and pointing it out in shallow water. Actually pointing,
three rings on her second finger, and saying nothing.

The body bloated,
feathers soft with scum from the lake.
Just its belly and one foot, rocking against incoming waves.

It moves past, under the dock, towards the neighbour's further south.

At least we didn't kill that one, I say.

Split Dinner

Cutting the steak in two and splitting the potatoes onto our plates.
White wine set beside her ankle, red next to my foot.

Swallows hopping across the beach with
crushed insects in their beaks.

Cut tomatoes layered onto meat.
Green beans.
Slicing down the centre.

I don't think I appreciate the lake enough, she says.

Construction Site

That elbow of beach on the way out to Ellison Park.
Used to come here, tunnelling through roadside scrub, to the water.

Ducks and geese scattering, honking and choking as they flee.
Now all of it turned over, all gravel and crushed stone.

At one time, the most beautiful stretch of pebbled beach
on the north end of the Okanagan.

Stumbling down to a felled tree, opening the beer.
No birds, now.

Sipping brandy from a canning jar.

Rubbing her neck and shoulders until my fingers are sore.
Building a wall for her to lean into.

Architecture of bodies beside the lake.

Poncho

Wait a second.

She stops, turns. Can't see her, but her voice as she calls back.
What?

Teeth into the woven cotton of my sleeve, dry bitter taste of cloth,
pulling at a three-inch ring of material and tearing this off.

Something to wipe with.

Thanks.

Finishing the brandy while she crouches between trees.
Ripping the same strip off the other sleeve and tucking this
into my back pocket.

Came here once before, with her and her sister and
a few other friends, to swim.
Watched them all run out,
silhouettes with bright white strips of ass,
laughing and crashing into the lake like crazed geese.

Or this time, hands over her black sweater and finding knots everywhere.
All the ropes woven into her back, pulling.
Fingers clawing at her spine,
pressing smooth down the back of her neck,
her head rolling forward and an almost unheard sound
that is both pain and release.

Ripping our clothes off, then. Now ripping them apart.

Sipping Beer

Driving back past where Mike and Betty used to live.
Where the Ross's used to live.

Past dry sand cliffs riddled with swallows' nest holes.
Clouds over the old car splitting like wake as we speed back.

Twisting along Okanagan Landing Road.
Two of her fingers resting on my wrist.

One hand on the gear-shift, one on a can of beer,
knee holding the wheel.

Flying back in the old car, not speaking, sipping beer.

Map of Stars

I fell out. Can't believe that. Didn't think I was that drunk,
maybe wasn't.

Spreading out the orange hammock, sitting down slowly,
yet lifting my left foot too soon and both of us laughing as I
end up at her feet.

She holds my arm as I get up, smiles in half light,
more off the lake than moon or stars.

Then both of us into it, slowly. Easily.

Side by side at first, then pulling her
carefully onto my chest, shoulder.

Both of us still looking up at a map of stars
broken by the continents of tree-tops.

Bare cottonwood.

Can hear the water next to us,
the slight squeal of bats.

Nothing to say, really.

Charting her body without touching.

North Okanagan shoulders,
smooth lake of stomach,
beautiful and ridiculous valleys.

Hammock

Help her off the hammock around two in the morning
after she says, I don't want to be a wiener but
I think I should go.

Walking with her to her tent as ducks gush in circles,
biting at tail-feathers.

Sleeve

Later, you pin it down,
like a bleached needle through the spine of a hummingbird,
pin the second strip of sleeve to the bookshelf
so she will not fly off.

Worry I'm falling apart,
joyous and breaking down.

Almost want to.

Mad loon diving too long for the glint of minnows,
insane to catch in beak, mouth.

Forgetting air.

If we could just forget how to speak

Like the newly deaf
a small chalk-board around our necks
so that I could write what will not find sound.

When you sit on the dock,
could tap out onto window
spell out

> I want to stand with our backs
> together   after undressing
> and reaching behind us
> explore each other like the blind

so that when you hear me come home
stepping into the boathouse
for paper, pencil

sound of my stepping onto
the beach   the dock
means I should be pulling into bed
with you   regardless
of blankets you might steal.

But I am a fool

afraid you might wake
we might speak.

Even the note you leave on the desk
this voice like your hand on my neck
that I know well.

Or your face that is the sound of you
to read like a letter.

Hate that I have a voice.

Grasp for chalk
to write

Am still numbed by you
Help me

You are asleep
in my bed
       while I sit on the dock.

Worry that it is only the idea of you.

How does anyone sleep.

Blue Tent

Wait three days for your message.

Red flash at the top of the hill,
the screech of bats over the lake.

Can see your tent from the end of the dock.

Habits of your candle.

Shift of your moving
in silhouette.

There are dogs
on the other side
that bark across Okanagan

to our side   unseen

gestures
that like secrets
are revealed as a shiver

a body's voice

returned by quail
bats   other animals.

♋

Can't see the stars tonight.

Big Dipper, 1982.
There.

Sleeping on the floating dock
when shoulders wouldn't feel this hard wood.

Tonight just cloud and the lake's quiet movement.

Content to hear this.

Feet resting in water.

♌

Leaving you a package two days ago:

blank postcard,
a worn copy of *Secular Love.*

These annotated notes
carried across lake shore
to be read next to your candle,
precarious in all our fury.

Returning the make-up bag
you'd left in the sand—
compact and lip balm—
after touching this
that your chin   lips   eyelids
have touched

then walked home in disguise.

Reflecting off the windows of cars
parked along the road.

Red lips laughing,

luckily.

♌

And how would she respond?

Conjure a blur of aurora.

Or throw willow boughs into the lake
after touching each leaf
with her fingertips.

Hold a cloth to her sex
to hang on the door
to find in the morning,
    the scent gone.

Cells in her body
that communicate
by destroying.

Messages lacking this horror of language.

Somewhere a lesson in this.

Go to bed.

꘎

Three nights ago
spelling out
onto the skin of your back:

We can never leave this tent

and your finger draws confusion
from the palm of my hand:

No.

Sound locked in a nylon room.

Then leaving.

Stepping from her tent
into morning
as birds already beginning
to rumour
murmur,

You can not go back.

Ω

Lamp lit and set
next to this chair
here, at the end of the dock.

A bat's sonar question
glancing off the calm lake.

Returned to it.

note left at her tent

another crazy night with Jack and now
half comma of hangover
can't help but want the simple ease
crib playing   soft spoken
quiet afternoon with you
if for no other reason
than a diversion from the easily regrettable
drunken nights on the beach

your sweet company in the slow afternoon

note left at the boathouse

You have been eating angels again—
I can see their feathers between your teeth.

This isn't fair to him.

I won't come again.

And when she's on a roll
she takes a razor from her boot,
and a thousand pigeons
fall around her feet.

Shit

postcard to a friend in Nagoya

Feel like one of those sucker frogs in grade-II biology, poker
rammed up its ass, chest and stomach slit open, held wide with pins,
bubbles of fat gushing out, raisin of heart, body jabbed and thrown
across the room

'hey debbie! catch!'

flying across desks
broken and useless
waiting to hit the wall.

Like a hand held under the surface of Okanagan Lake

In the sandhills below cliff swallows' nests,
you remember reading the biology of quicksand

each grain
   perfect
   round as loose water.

Weight of foot or hand
sinking slow into sand, so that
any movement to lift
becomes an act of drowning.

♒

You decide today to organize
   to find order.
Books scattered and bottles beside the bed.

Cutting pieces of hair in the boathouse,
dropping these to the floor,
mirror drunk with steam,

   and this is like shaving
at seven a.m.,
aware of angles of jaw   and blade.

Sun through the window
like light under water

(blue flame glowing from the old Coleman stove).

℧

Overcompensating the shedding fig tree,

  you fill two bottles with water
and pour this
through dry browning leaves.

Expect miracles of green.

The skin of insects
on the edge of lake.

Water spilling out the bottom
in streams onto the floor.

Or sand at the bottom of the lake
rich with rot and algae.

Feet into this and cold
between toes   pushing against
the weightlessness of body.

℈

    Glimmer of sky
on the underside of surface.

Hands waving through thick wet.

A face an inch away
from air
  watching air.

A cliff swallow choking on grasshopper as
its cave nest collapses.

The new sand
cold between feathers.

Morning Swim

The geese today, along the beach and up onto hard summer grass, twisting beaks into wings, preening. Every morning they begin north, up the lake shore, and by noon are strewn along the edge of the water here, or resting on the dock, littering it with plucked feathers and soft green shit. Have learned, through a kind of necessity and admiration, two ways of walking past them: a loud, hard step out of sand and onto the pier, storming ahead, to get them back into water. *Get th'hell off'th* . . . Smiling. Or slow careful steps, keeping eye contact and speaking softly. Always one or two of the thicker, stronger males standing fast, black feet firm on driftwood or a rock for height. Watching me, carefully. And sensing no threat, signalling for the others to come back. That it's safe.

Out on the dock this morning in the sleeping bag. These old rituals this summer. Wake around ten, when shadow off the roof is halfway across the fire pit. Out into hot sun in the late morning with the sleeping bag, bottle of Naya water and cigarettes. Cocooned thick in the down blanket over the rotting wooden slats of the floating pier. Hot white sun blinding at first, then revealing blue, then the even whiter bellies of darting swallows that still worry me. That summer when I was eleven and they'd built a nest in one of the piles that hold the dock. Diving a thousand miles an hour at my head neck shoulders. Never colliding, but almost.

They seem to like Nina Simone. Another ritual. While cooking eggs around noon I look out to see they are learning new tricks today. Just past cottonwoods and the willow up the beach, there are ten or fifteen of them. Then, suddenly, a dozen more burst out of the water like beachballs held on the bottom with awkward feet. Some throwing themselves sideways, turning over, black feet kicking through the surface of the lake, then righting themselves. Flapping

31

their wings, almost lifting out into air. Resting. Adjusting feathers. Then diving again. Learning to swim for minnows like loons and grebe. Forcing their thick bodies in, diving, snapping at slender silver. Resurfacing.

Years since I spent a summer here in this small cabin on the Okanagan. Yet slipping back into these routines. After first cigarette and bottle of water, pulling off my shorts beneath the blanket, lazy, then standing, pushing, toes on the last plank, up, off the dock. Arching down and pulling into cold. Stretching out within it. The water a cold hand raking down the length of body, waking me. Then onto the pier to watch the geese, a hundred yards down the beach, as they approach.

Some days, if I sit still, a few will end up next to me, ten, fifteen feet away, confident before I stand and wave them off the dock.

This summer different though. Toronto, Victoria, New York. Four years away from Vernon. Forgot this alone here, although pleased to find the lake birds stars blue sun still here. Still patient and willing. The thick patterned body of spider that has built his thin house over one pane of the front window. Some Grimm's character, watching me in the evenings when the lamp is on to keep him warm. *She's not coming*, he says each night. *You're stuck with us.* Not stuck though, not exactly. Not like that tiny moth under your legs you're sucking on. More like the goslings that feed amongst the reeds and muck on the beach. Wings growing slowly, thick black and grey feathers pushing out of yellowgrey fur. Rebuilding.

Content to move back and forth from the lake to the cabin. Touch wood, sand, grass. Dance to Nina Simone while cooking breakfast.

Move amongst these heavy birds while they bathe.

Thick blue, glinting. Cracking into it, black at first, then sparkling phosphorescent under eyelids as cold green moves down over shoulders ribs testicles thighs feet. Then up, pulling with hands into green, two three times pulling, then up, smooth, into air while blue then green of hills and colours of houses, boats, sky. Back towards the dock for soap, toothbrush. My morning swim.

The geese on the next pier north of the cabin towards Kin Beach, watching me.

Géricault's Severed Limbs Paintings

The best argument for Beauty
as it ought to be understood.
                —Eugene Delacroix

Listen. If I have known beauty
let's say I came to it
asking
                —Phyllis Webb

Pictorial realism alone did not require him to turn his studio into a morgue,
which he did for some weeks. Without making himself a complete cannibal,
he familiarized himself with the sights and smells of death, and tried to live
with it day by day.

His friend Lebrun, who had retired to the village of Sevres to recover from
an attack of jaundice which had so disfigured him that he terrified passers-by
in the street, was met one day by Géricault, who greeted him with the cry:
'How beautiful you are,' and with a hug, pressed him to pose for a portrait.

—Lawrence Eitner
Géricault's Raft of the Medusa

To Lebrun he said it was all very simple.
The rumours were ridiculous. He wasn't mad.
He simply wanted to understand.

The studio scattered with objects.

On a table near the window
two legs, severed above the knee, tangled
as feet beneath sheets
rubbing together before sleep

held, *intimate*
    —a casual embrace
    or clinging to hold—
by an arm cut off at the collar bone

    and Géricault
pouring alcohol over fragments each day
to keep the flesh clean and damp
to slow and *observe a gradual decay.*

When your hand, cut off in shadow,
moves shapeless
spreading fingers woven into my hair,

simple gesture twisting absently as words,

   or your mouth
that I have not seen opened up
and so for now, at least,
have left unquestioned.

Or
     sucking your own tongue
when you are almost asleep

thtick thtick of yet born heart
still wet in multiple skins
and liquid rhythmic,

you are almost too alive.

There are a handful of entrance wounds
towards autopsy
and each anomaly
leads to others

    Once found
all incisions are redundant,
flippant.

It seems as though it would be obvious
how at one time
these pieces made up various wholes—
bodies or ideas, images.

That foot on the desk,
a head set on the work bench
that he's faced down,
feeling secretive or
at least private.

Worried, at times,
when he would sit next to the window
and the scent
   not of body
but bodies
sifting past him,

an *argument for beauty.*
Disputing nechrophilia,

and forgetting, again,
to eat.

When you clutch at my necklace
as for a rope in water
            and say
I won't let you leave

and taking your thumb, slowly,
I fold it into your palm

knowing your fingers
    despite anger, stubborn want,
will shoot release

a sharp, sudden pain
you didn't expect,
grasping, cannibal, towards body.

The trick is to move
thoughtless
towards this small assault
as towards a caress,

then to slip into the walk home
as three hours earlier
I promised I would.

You tell me afterward
I have it all wrong.

You have not, in fact,
been lying as I was so sure,

have managed, in fact, to escape
these linguistic contortions, you say,
while spilling truths
    inadvertently
all over me.

Drawing your body with lines

Disturbed, lacking sleep,
an open pocket knife
    unexpectedly sharp
lifting thin red welts
traced along skin

Cringing as it follows the scar
down your wrist

or from the hollow of navel
splitting just the warmth of belly
following the "yum-yum trail"

a steadiness of heart and eye
in the face of an almost
unbearable reality.

Hands that crinkle into fists and
bat at her head in protest or joy.
She bites her lip at the moment,
claims it this way,
with a tiny incision
and a little blood she wipes away with her sleeve.

Can you feel me trembling when you do that?

          Can you
feel me do that
when you're trembling?

India ink
Cigarettes
'Raft of the Medusa' coasters

The Art of Vivisection
Ideology

Green tea

X-acto blades

Or when you've left
and the warmth of your hand
on my sleeve

shape of your neck
imprinted on pillow

or your breast
that has left its taste
fervent, in my mouth.

Pieces of you scattered, rampant,
throughout the apartment
turning these rooms into morgue.

Reflecting on your coffee with sugar
your tortured fingernails

your thin
thin arms.

Dissecting a new desire.

This all but cadaverous rapture,
conjuring a morbid curiosity.

Arranging them again on the table,

cold in the studio
and his hand slips over wet skin,

thumb pushing into
open.

And lifting this to his mouth,
glancing across the room
for witness,

tasting.

Or losing, for the moment,
the reason of this touching,
and instead
following the contour of sex
as diagram.

Two, three fingers
pushed into you,
and your broken breath
an exclamation to this
discovering.

Or slicing the web of skin between fingers,
a blade of paper drawn across tongue
to take you wet, metallic salt
stinging into thin cuts,
and dissolve you
cellular.

As though you have been slaughtered,
the scent of you lingers in these rooms
for hours after you leave.

If there is to be any clarity at all,
it demands a certain assiduity.

I stand on the bed,
head thrown back

and inhaling deeply
    ask my questions this way.

moving to the clear

Badlands

Not until a Drumheller hotel room do we begin to presume.

Breaking apart the bed table
to hold the window open,
you, wearing purple men's briefs,
    your drink on the sill
    threatened by passing trains,
hold out your hand as an answer
like those women who,
    lowering their heads,
    allowed or deigned their lovers,
and putting your mouth to my eye
            taste sand dust.

A mile west this town does not exist.
The ground swallows it,
holds it beneath a wall of sand a hundred feet deep,
    everything bone under it.

Leaning from the window
yelling at the sign you can't reach,
one hand holding the back of my neck.

We have given up playing cards.

One of us may fall out and
I'm not kidding.

Hawk on the street light
tears the throat out of a field-mouse.

                    We talked about going further,
had another drink
before the heat destroyed
larynx, as though fevered.

Didn't speak of it again.

After the hoodoos east of Rosedale,
worn smooth as your hip by wind,
we put our clothes back on,
and shaking sand into the heat before we left
        buried our footprints.

Moving to the clear

Outside Rachel and Jenna's voices curl like insects around the trees, slip as though carried on wind around the porch, yet caught sharp as Jenna trips on the wet grass; a small shriek as mud slips apart and her foot lifts momentarily weightless into air. Ankle stretching to find the ground, gone. Index finger pushing into grass, folded over other fingers, rampant to find a hold as her knees catch on her skirt, thrust taut into the wet lawn, absorbing thick mud. All of this instantaneous: a glint of sun through the wings of monarch, less than a second of sudden stained glass refracted across the yard before anyone notices. Lost or missed in the burst of sparks that explode from the fire. And then laughter. Jeremy throws himself down too, onto his hands and knees, claws at the grass like a cat kneading through jeans or sweater, almost purring and out of breath. The two of them looking up at each other before springing to their feet. The other kids still turning in a kind of circle, yet running awkward and shapeless around the yard, chasing after and running from each other simultaneously. And away from them a wave of sound that like water folds at different levels, carrying or reflecting everything around it, expanding out and touching the trees, the shed, the adults on the porch. Even from the slightly opened window I can hear this.

On the porch Joe eyes them over the railing. He has the stern face of an old Italian, yet hides a smile that the kids see without looking. He has watched them grow up over the past seven years, sitting on this porch each summer when Jeff has the staff barbecue. The one time each year that Joe shows up. Tyla and Danika take turns sitting on his lap, flirting as they do with him at work, holding their plastic cups of beer precarious to his mouth. Linda, sitting next to him, has grown used to this as well. The girls are only a few years older than Clifford, yet Joe warms to their attention easily. Reserves the bite of his observation from the two of them and, bouncing his knee, bumps them away. As Jenna's knees push into wet grass behind him he admires Jeremy's gesture, and his hand, thoughtless, reaches for Linda's. He has a jaw that could cut glass.

Jeff stands at the barbecue wearing the apron Alexa's brought for him. His face a spattering of lipstick as each arriving guest has taken him up on the *kiss the cook* logo. He turns to see Danika slip off Joe's lap, catching herself quickly and saving her beer. Smiles as he sees Mark and Laura coming from the master bedroom, admiring the new bed. A cheer goes up as they step through the patio doors, glasses finding the table quickly as hands reach for Laura's belly. She is nothing but radiant with a sore back, smiling towards everyone around the picnic table as Mark pulls his fingertips, lightly, across her nape in front of him. From the terra-cotta oven a log cracks, throws sparks up over the yard and Jeff turns quickly to see Jenna slip in the wet grass. The spatula pausing in air, he holds a hamburger in mid-flip as he waits for either laughter or a wail to swell up towards the porch. And he turns to Laura and smiles as Jenna leaps back into the fray. They have been trying to get pregnant for over a year. Jeff remembers Shelly's belly smooth above bath water, her navel that looked so sore, and his hand circling over her, warm.

Jacob runs his hand slowly over his head, feels the close-cropped strands fanning out beneath his fingers. A small cut on his knuckle that still stings from helping Shelly cut tomatoes and cilantro into the salsa. Pouring in some Cuervo from above the stove. Steve, abandoned to the porch, is comfortable with these people now. Has gotten to know them while waiting for Jacob after work as they all sit in the empty restaurant doing their cash. After rinsing his hands, Jacob follows Mark and Laura onto the porch, notices Mark's hand and walks past them to Steve. Steps around his chair and slips his fingers, cold from the tap water, under the collar of Steve's shirt. Feels the muscles of his back shiver to the touch and lets his palm slide across Steve's shoulder as he sits in the chair next to him. They are leaving in three weeks for England.

Tyla and Zena sit on the porch steps and shout encouragement to the kids. Tyla holds a wineglass on her knee and fingers her necklace. She can see, through the laughter and smile towards the girls running wild, the concern in Zena's eyes. Tyla's attention drawn away from the back yard as Mark and Laura arrived, Zena's shoulders pulling up suddenly at the uproar as she stepped over Tyla's knees, unaware of their entrance and frozen for a second as though waiting for a stray golf ball to drill into her back. Looking back to see the scramble for Laura and carefully finding her footing on the steps. Watching as Zena sits down beside her, surveying the yard hesitantly, Tyla is aware of what she is looking for. *He's been running around with the kids for the last hour. Looks like he's about to pass out from trying to keep up with them. I think he has a crush on Jenna.* And Zena's smile is only half forced. She is fairly new at the restaurant and is still a little unsure of the kindness she's found herself in. More so of Tyla as she was seeing him not long ago. Knows there is something she's not telling. And him, leaving in a few days after only three nights. Zena's feet twitch as Jenna slips in front of them, about to jump towards accident as the young girl bolts away towards the others. Antigonish is 3,000 miles away.

I can hear her hand lifting the wineglass to her lips, this movement carried by the current of the girls' voices as they drift in through the open window. Yet this is not a sound but a substance that like water spills in through the window with the lightness and volume of air. A hand that, thoughtless, can lift this fallen girl from wet grass, or reach beyond the rhetoric and blur of words. My back against the wall of the bathroom beneath the window, crouching next to the counter as sun catches and glints through clear glass, through clear liquid as though looking up towards the surface of a lake. My head back and resting against the wall. Staggering from the back yard with Jenna and

Rachel tied to my legs by their thin arms, heaving their small weight and trying to smile. *I'll be right back, I promise. But where are you going?* Looking up to see Jeff on the porch, concern in his eyes too   *I have to go the __bath__room*   and Zena walking out onto the porch just as their arms spill me, suddenly light, towards the door   *Well, __hurry up__!* their voices calling as I stumble towards the basement   and almost sick, can feel myself almost sick as I grab my backpack next to the door rush into the bathroom   crouch beneath the window and slice my finger on the cap   hands shaking   twisting it off   vodka stream-ing down over my chin   my neck   hadn't noticed the nausea while chasing the kids   and drunk for years at this point   Jenna's hand on mine for only a second   too fragile   awful   and suddenly guilt rolling over me   lurching away from this touch   the enormity of its innocence   the simple touch of a small hand   one instant as ocean   sick in the bathroom looking up through clear glass and liquid and swallowing as much and as fast as I can   half the bottle gone as Jenna slips and rights herself in the back yard.

Observations Midway Through October

I

Today my father comes to visit, his face warm but
crooked with concern. I am busy with classes, distracted.
These days my heart is set, blue plum in a bowl.
In this cold wind autumn moves slowly,
each leaf hesitating its silent undress. At night
the tea steams with air that twists the candle flame.
Most nights I sleep well, the bed warming slowly.
I have not, in over a month, had a drink. And
my hands, although at times not empty, notice
your absent chin. The cat sits in the window,
swallows the scent of those walking past, his eyes
fearless. My father carries a tomato, in his
briefcase, a thousand kilometres from his garden,
and gives me this.

2

Our conversation is interrupted at times, on the couch,
as chestnuts fall and break, green husk a body, splitting
on the sidewalk outside. Footprints along windowsill,
the cat's feet after stepping over the potted fig. Laughing
when I mutter into the kitchen to reheat the tea.
You have been visiting often, late into the night.
Ashtray filled quickly. Other interruptions.
Leaves that follow rash suicides, a mute comment
on stalled talk. Outside they ride the air regardless,
as insects searching out warmth inside the tree body.
You cannot spend the night.

3

This is a weather for jackets. Pencil stub left
in a pocket months ago. Burgundy leather and the old
sheepskin in case of rare winter, waiting in the hall
closet, eager for purpose. At night the cars lift rain
from the ground and throw this demented into air,
hissing. Have been staying up late. Listening.
Thinking of my grandfather again, that old coat, another
absent winter, skin unable to cling to metal blade, to tear
this away. Fleshing my flesh clean to be sewn.
Pockets where forgotten items are found.

4

My scars expand when I breathe, my skull expands. I am still
sending postcards, occasionally, to that Colombian girl. Stand
with my hand on the radiator and imitate thermometer,
the other hand held out into this room. Cold air from the window
twitching on veins of my wrist, vibration of a spider's strewn gut
telling stories, or walking to the store for coffee,
air that smells like sitting outside in this cold, the taste of whiskey
that warms like the first touched body. I stop
in front of the mirror, trying to get a handle on my face,
muscles of my eyebrows I flex now with conceit, my
grandfather's creases settling into my forehead.
May or may not go insane and walk the length of Siberia.

Our ongoing argument on representation

You buy a full-length mirror at a garage sale
and set it against your wall in the bathroom.

    An experiment, you say
There's something I want to see.

And standing before it
still as photograph,
you break down
this view of that self.

Then call with description:

How under the skin of shoulder
bone juts ugly against the receiver.
Left foot kicking, gangly, at the wall.
Scar on the inside of your knee.
Crease of thigh that frames your sex.

You've stopped bleeding and
your breasts are back to normal.

You have discovered, you say, a new language
in the grand deformity of body.

Terrible as sculpture.

At a party when you were thirteen
you set down your drink in the kitchen,
stood looking at yourself in the window

and pushing your hands through the glass
drew the outline of a woman
on the skin of your wrists.

Told me on our first date,
you are not allowed to touch me here.

You have asked me to be more direct about my feelings

Your letter, first picked up by a draft from the window,
is blown off the desk and drifts down to the rug behind me.
The cat watches it land, then bolts from the room.

Last night, the moon bright onto the bed,
I woke to find him curled against my stomach,
his weight warm over the blanket,
my hand open against the soft fur of his belly, and
his expression of almost embarrassed violation as he recognized that
I thought he was someone else.

I have removed the insects from the glass box they were mounted in
and have sealed them individually in small glass jars.
When I turn off the lamp at night, on my way from the desk to the bed,
the green metallic phosphorescence of their shells glow, if only for a
second, as bright green flames.
He has not discovered them yet.

He sits, for extended periods of time, feeling the new warmth as the
radiator pops and clangs to life. Autumn. A breeze from the window
making this heat somehow thicker. Sits observing the plant my sister gave
me years ago as a housewarming gift, its slow decline as the radiator
cooks its roots, the leaves falling dry around the planter, browning, the
stems splitting and drooping. Occasionally he glances towards the desk
where I am reading. Wonders, I think,
when I will notice this unobtrusive death scene.

In the kitchen he has begun an exchange with the CBC.
Sits facing the wooden box on which the radio is set, above his food dish,
and gives voice to his opinions. When I come home sometimes I can hear
him before the jingle of keys alerts him to my approach, or when,
still for hours reading, he grows tired of my ignoring him and forgets
that I am here at all. A strange sort of gurgled argumentative ramble that
he inserts between segments of *As It Happens* or *The Afternoon Show*.
A request for more musical programming, or maybe an appeal for the
return of Vicki Gabareau. When I walk into the kitchen for more Coke he
looks at me as though I have rudely interrupted his conversation.

In the morning he sits on the toilet and cries while I'm in the shower.
He does not understand this self-abuse.

When he is particularly hungry he will move as panther across the room,
slip beneath the bookshelf and coil himself as python around my ankle.
He has learned, somehow, a stealth of touch that allows him the ability
to do this without detection. Then, as crocodile, he lingers, motionless,
beneath the surface of the desk. Waits until I adjust my position to
reach for a cigarette or turn on the printer, uses this movement to set his
claws. Drives his jaw into my shin
and takes what he feels he has due.

At other times he sits on the rug in the middle of the room behind me.
Just sits there.
Then begins to scream.

Undressing for bed

In the hall, an echo of rain
slings around doorway
from the window
in the bedroom.

Have just turned out the bathroom light
and shape grows out of dark.
Risk of certain corners
other, unseen obstacles.

Three summers ago
you plucked a sudden tree-frog
from the bed table
and set it, kingly
on your naked hip
and air, cool off the lake
slipped in through the window,
        made this wet touch   more.

Wiped your fingers on the sheet
and said *Which one of us will leave first?*

Now, in the hallway, spattered
by the rain's tapping.
Droplets that weave as drunk
and find me naked between rooms.

                    Here
at the tip of elbow, lower stomach
neglected desire of hands.
Locations of anamnetic touch
where impossible rain
lands as too-remembered fingertips
still amphibian wet.

As though that air ripple
has found me here,
suspended or reeling
on the way to bed.

In Theory

Yuri Tynyanov ponders another relationship gone bad

*'Creative freedom' thus becomes
an optimistic slogan which does not correspond to reality,
but yields instead to the slogan
'creative necessity.'*

By my own logic it should be clear / this
progression of events / is convention / that
I have little to do with / if anything.
And yet I sit now / wondering what form
your absence is to take / this time.

Shape of body missing from bath water / or
in other moments of weakness / writing you
into these rooms. / A scent caught in air
as I come from the kitchen / to sit
at this desk / and then gone. / Absorbed.

And what is the logic of this / what?
lack of deformity? / This sequence yet again.
A needed deviation to acts / kept static
too long. / *What?* you scream / backing out the door
What are you trying to say?

That I'm stuck? / That your leaving is necessary?
A mutation / as is needed now
in order to attempt this / shapeless. / Cracked
or swollen / into substance. / Content
of the space behind the bones of my breast.

There is no form / without content,
you say. / A heart useless with theoretical gestures.
A thousand baths run / a thousand
times the thought to run your bath. / And now regret
it seems / becomes function.

I have exercised an image too long. / Sculpting you,
creating you at night / as you slept.
All the things you are not. / A freedom, really
that now with a breeze from the window
necessitates creation to reclaim your absent touch.

Jacques Derrida reconsiders the stricture of definition

It is not, as I may have thought in the past,
only an alteration of pattern;
a new telling of another story
told now with a voice unfamiliar, yet known—
nor is it a rediscovery of object
lost years ago
or placed ceremoniously into a wooden box
made quietly in the December cold of some Alberta
where I have set certain memories to be taken up again
in moments of reflection, or loss—
and neither is it a matter of waking to sunlight
or the violence of storm against the window at night
    all of these are types of recapitulation;
simply a retracing of footsteps on a perpetually buried path
as snow or time erases the imprint of travel, experience—

and it is not a retreat, as I had thought till now;
not a succumbing to release,
or a slip into the renewed grace of trust—
yet it is also not a negation of history
to recreate a lost certainty, innocence
but rather, it is as though the knowledge I had
was simply, yet utterly
incomplete.

"The air cannot hold such / intensity,
another heart couldn't possibly understand."

And so these moments
when I am not ruined by question,
my heart, instead, forgets itself
and it is your heart I feel, here
with a hand to my chest.

And air is not rediscovered
but is born here, new.

It is as though
until now
I had never
taken
a breath.

A letter from Victor Shklovsky to his lover

after the Victoria earthquake, December 11, 1999

Want to get this down
before time and movement take us further along.

Already the arbitrary threat of habit:
running out of milk in the morning,
or the shower out of hot water
for the third day in a row.

These are crucial hours,
    words from a year ago, held
and carried by a tremor in air. This letter
slipped into the sleeve of your coat,
to be found later, *everything balanced,*
delicately, precariously, just out of reach.

    A year later, this rain,
normal I guess.

Outside the street is streaming towards you,
currenting over November leaves.

Last year at this time
I hadn't spoken to you in months.

And tonight I worry the abstraction of pattern.

(It's only a tremor...)

That I might catch the skin of your sex with the scissors.
That you will be offended. That you will begin to notice my legs
trembling as we stand on the bed.
That my hand at your throat,
which surprised even me as your breath became rapid,
will become not anticipated, but expected.
That we will dissolve into silence, again.
That our movements will habituate into language,
away from a metaphor of speaking,
from your hand that takes my hand, says, here.

That I will forget what you have asked me.
That we will forsake the awkward fumbling of morning
for the dialogue of routine. That what is left of my CDs,
after the robbery, will grow tiresome, repetitive.
That the smoke from our cigarette, curling into light
from the window, will settle in the air above the bed, and hold us still,
broken, into the deaf insensibility of sleep.

It is a testament to the uselessness of speech that I am certain
you are awake beside me at five AM Even without the message of gesture
I am sure of your awareness. Of the gentle tremor that begins in the
heart, stomach, in the organs of body, like the shiver of your orgasm
that I feel in the palm of my hand on your spine. Our skin
taking on this quivering and seizing into awareness. Your fingers
that suddenly find my wrist, curling like claws into panic.

It moves out from our stillness into the room until the walls themselves
are trembling, the window shuddering in its sill, and then this structure
groans out a release that settles within seconds into stillness.

For a night, at least, the stasis of encroaching habit
is thwarted by the anticipation and terror of disaster.

As though the shudder of our earlier coming
has found its way into the ground, three stories below,
and has forced us awake to feel its insistence.

In the morning you have left various voices behind you:
CBC from the kitchen detailing the night's distraction,
two pages on the bed table.

So I reach, again, for pen, paper,
hoping that this time I'll give you something clear,
not these fragments of ideas, feelings.

Our attempts at construct, to offer a context
of desire, meaning. Cluttered in what I can only describe
as poetry, blurred by the risk of misinterpretation.

For now we exist somewhere on an edge, somewhere
between speaking and listening, giving and taking,
tasting each moment and dissolving into this.

These written messages, still exchanged in silence,
that we do not mention in daylight, if ever. No longer a sequence
of responses to previous attempts at explanation, but a body,
constantly mutating points of reference,
conditioned, always, by motion, the body's shudder, earthquake.

So these words, as any allowed to escape our lips,
are put into the other's hands, trusted
to be interpreted.

Offered as gifts as wet ink on the page.

Mikhail Bakhtin abandons us on the High-Level Bridge

I

The sound of the stove as you roast jalapenos over blue flame,
clink of the cat's collar on his dish next to your feet,
the dry scratching of pages while I sit on the couch reading Bakhtin.

Books screeching on the desk in the other room.

There are too many voices filling the apartment.

Like a crowd gathered in these rooms,
they demand to be heard.

Or later, biting my sweater,
the sound of your teeth against cotton.

Despite my complaints of too much to read, you are pleased,
you say, that I no longer know where these words are leading,
so that we are, at least, on similar paths.

Besides, you say,
there are better things to be done with our tongues.

2

Arriving back from the SAVE-ON
laughing with our hands filled with bags,
there is an argument spilling out of #4.

A car wreck of voices, tearing through air like shrapnel,
a crushing explosion as the apartment is torn apart,
and the sound of a child, screaming.

Before we can move, the girl appears on the stairs,
runs half-way up and stops, her small chest heaving,
her hands held trembling over her mouth,
unaware of our presence, three steps away.

We are afraid even to breathe.

That she might hear us.

Another voice.

3

Later that night, on the bridge, there is no sound at all.

Cars rush past in silence.
I can not even hear myself breathe.

Only the voice of wind, pooling in our ears like water and
moving through us without question,
high above the river.

Even our feet make no sound,
as though we were not, really,
touching the ground at all.

4

Like the fan turned on at night, next to the bed,
so that these rooms hum with steady movement,
a ghost voice like liquid in the air around us,

refusing the maelstrom of language

while we, in agreement,
open our mouths
just enough
for our tongues
to touch.

JASON DEWINETZ grew up in the Okanagan Valley of British Columbia and, after living in Victoria, Toronto, Paris, New York, and Edmonton, has now settled back in Victoria. A graduate of the University of Victoria (Hons. BA) and the University of Alberta (MA), he is the founding editor of Greenboathouse Books, and organizer of The Greenboathouse Reading Series, held annually in Vernon, British Columbia.

Acknowledgements

To John Lent. Ben Alway. The two Dianes. Suzanne Buffam and Judy MacInnes Jr. Sveva Caetani. D.M. Thomas. Julie Oakes. Nancy, Sharon, Kate, and Anni Lawrence. Pauline Yablonski. Jay Ruzesky, Harold Rhenisch, and Derk Wynand. Laisha Rosnau and Noah Buchan. Lisa Miloy. Amelia Barker. Eva Moran. Natali, Danny, Tyla, and Danika. My mom, dad, Sanci, and Erik. My editor, Doug Barbour, as well as Ruth and Erin at NeWest. And Zena. Thank you.